CHAPTERS OF ME
DEEP THOUGHTS VOL.1

BEN HINSON

MUSINGS PRESS™

MUSINGS PRESS™

2011

CHAPTERS OF ME: *DEEP THOUGHTS VOL.1*

By **Benjamin Hinson-Ekong**

www.benhinson.com

facebook.com/BenHinson2

Published by Musings Press, LLC.

P.O Box 8718

New York, NY. 10116

Printed in the United States of America.

Library of Congress Control Number:

ISBN: 978-0-615-52109-1

Book layout by Sylvia Ayivor

www.edemdesignstudio.com

Cover design by Stella Lillig

www.stellalillig.com

Printed in the United States of America

ACKNOWLEDGEMENTS

Art in its entirety takes on many forms of expression – sound, move-ment, images, words...it takes an open mind to appreciate the beauty in them all.

Many thanks to God; my wife and beautiful daughter; my Aunt Marjorie; my buddy Stella for the hookup; Stephen Ceneus for assisting me with shooting my videos; the few wise men and women I've met and listened to on all my travels; any good person in my life who has actively and genuinely supported me; and the beautiful people on that continent someone named Africa.
And finally, I thank you the reader for granting me an audience ☺

— Ben

CONTENTS

Acknowledgements   3

For My People   10

Beautiful Things   11

Moving   13

Poetry   15

Round 2   16

Bitches   18

Morning   19

The System   20

King   22

Jackie   23

New York   24

Masks   27

Loser   28

Skin   29

Peace   30

Perceptions   31

Search Engines   32

C Train Uptown   33

Random Thoughts...   34

Warrior   35

New York Playboy   36

Beautiful Music   37

Wannabe Rapper   38

Opportunity   39

My Resume   40

Hard Guy   42

Just Chillin'   43

Fantasy   44

Fake Mo'fo   45

I Learn   46

Nerd   47

Peaceful   48

Random Thoughts...   49

The Graveyard   50

My Brother   51

Weapons   52

Token 53

Single Story 56

The Future 57

Pain 58

Ignorance 59

Big Red Button On Her Forehead 60

Life Changes 61

Lenny 63

Wordplay 64

Hungry 65

Bredren 66

Knowledge Increases Your
Capacity To Be A Fool 67

Fingerprints 68

Immigrant 69

Jerry 70

Evening 71

Bubble With Hard Walls 72

Rose 73

Edem 74

The Foolish Man 76

Love 77

Kid 78

Trouble 79

Mind 80

Cocaine 81

Random Thoughts... 82

11 Kinds Of People
You'll Meet In Most Offices 83

Changes 85

Do You Believe 86

Little Fingers 88

Veil 89

Tongue 90

Plastic 91

The Road 92

Aftermath 93

Chump 94

Fabric Of Society 95

Original 96

I dedicate this collection to my dear friend Lartey; a smart, humble, classy man
with a good heart who has been nothing but a blessing to my family.

And to my Aunt Jackie,
One of the most peaceful women I have ever known.
R.I.P

CHAPTERS OF ME
DEEP THOUGHTS VOL.1

FOR MY PEOPLE

I've been writing for a long time till the present day

Call me a veteran – I know the alchemy of wordplay

Insecurities made me ask why I share my mind

External factors suggested I'm wasting my time

Never studied the art of poetry or prose

I'm just a common man sharing a few things he knows

Never received awards and I'm not acclaimed

My resume is called life and I've experienced the game

I used to be in a shell, but now I fly

Broke out of my fears like a butterfly

Previously thought like an ignoramus

Yes I admit, I wanted to be famous

Seeking positive opinions

Emotionally giving up my kingdom

Can't control what people think

So I gave up being my own personal shrink

Decided to lyrically portray the vibes in your mind

Tune you into my station so we'll be one of a kind

I wrote this for you because you are my people

And if I like how this goes I'll write a sequel

Art from the heart because tomorrow is not guaranteed

What good is treasure to a man when he's dead and can't breathe?

So sit back, relax and enjoy the show

Please be my audience as I share a few things I know.

—*July 18th 2011. 12:08a.m.*

BEAUTIFUL THINGS

Beautiful, like the way my daughter smiles at me

Beautiful, like getting something expensive for free

Beautiful, like getting over a cold and a sneeze

Or sitting on a beach and enjoying a beautiful breeze

Beautiful, like a good man getting praise for what he's done

Beautiful, like offering help and not being seen by anyone

Beautiful, like seeing two opposites get along

Like watching a choir made of different people

All sing the same song

Beautiful, like having people support you genuinely

Beautiful, like watching haters suddenly become friendly

Beautiful, like seeing gang rivals exchange hugs

Beautiful, like getting insulted and responding with a simple shrug

Beautiful, like listening to an old wise man talk

Or seeing the joy on a cripple's face who can suddenly walk

Beautiful, like watching little children play

They've not been corrupted by life, so for them everything's okay

Beautiful, like seeing a happy couple married for many years

Their love's been tested so you know that they really care

Beautiful, like being around a good person who's not just nice

A person can be evil, and still be very polite

Beautiful, like being very hungry and then getting food

Beautiful, like using laughter to cure a really bad mood

Beautiful, like making money after being poor for many years

The money tastes even sweeter because it was never there

Beautiful, like not worrying about the future but loving today

Unnecessary stress makes hairs turn grey

Beautiful, like having lovers also be best friends
Beautiful, like seeing a task through till the very end
Beautiful, like remembering to be grateful every single day
This life has too many distractions, which is why we pray
Beautiful, like understanding why a person does what they do
A life full of experiences will influence a point of view
Beautiful, like walking away from trouble
Beautiful, like watching a powerful man choose to be humble
Beautiful, like watching someone positive be influential
Beautiful, like observing a wordsmith at his craft with nothing but an
instrumental
Beautiful, like playing or repeating a powerful verse that was heard
Constructed with deliberately placed adjectives and verbs
These are just a few of the beautiful things I see
Beautiful, because they are nothing but unique to me

— *December 27th, 2011. 11:35a.m.*

MOVING

I keep it moving
Everyday steady improving
I don't live my life in rewind
I make use of my mind because there really isn't much time
In other words everyday I'm living in my prime
It's no coincidence, this is God's design
Everyday's never the same
New ideas filter through this thing called my brain
I don't mind the haters when they come through
They flap their gums wishing they could do the things that I do
They don't support my cause,
I give a speech but they look at me with no applause
That's okay because I keep it moving.
Dust the hate of my back and I keep improving
I wish you could understand
I am a method man
All because I have a plan, otherwise known as a vision
I'm pure energy that leaves a lasting impression
They know who I am but they don't say hello
May even see me suffering but there's no love that they show
I keep it moving; don't mind the people and their attitudes
In this life you can't control the things that people do
Like these chumps who try to mess my name
Inadequate bums who go on smear campaigns
I keep it moving, despite the good or bad
Life's too short and there's too much to be had

So when you see me show some love, don't be withdrawn
Because I'm like a breeze that comes,
And then it's gone
I keep it moving.

—*October 21st, 2011. 10:03p.m.*

POETRY

What the heck is poetry anyway?
I read once that poetry is:
"The art of rhythmical composition,"
"The art or craft of writing verse,"
"Literature given to the expression of feelings..."
Emotional writing infused with meaning.
The best form of communication, the simplest kind
Translating complex concepts to suit every mind
So I'll write my words and I will express myself
In whatever form I choose because it comes from self
Select groups will hate it. Arrogant minds can't do simple
My gift not to the exclusive,
But to all my people.

—July 23rd, 2011. 7:36pm.

ROUND 2

He got knocked down with a left hook he didn't see coming
He thought he could make it through the first round without running

But his opponent was fierce, caught him as he side stepped
Fake friends sold him out as he tried his best with nothing left

Testing ideas but no support comes
He failed the first time so fake friends run

They won't train with him
<u>But they will show if he wins</u>

He's down on the mat, referee starts to count
He gets on one knee as the pain starts to mount

They say it gets lonely as a man gets to the top
The pain of facing this reality is much,
And he wants it to stop

His trainer in his corner, yelling for him to stand if he can
In this life only a few people will really give a damn

He wants to give up, as the fans laugh at him
They call him a loser and say he can never win

Laugh at his first attempt and to him it stings
Won't even give him props for simply being in the ring

The referee continues to count, and his body shakes
So many people desert him, how much can he really take?

Sees his family in the crowd, they believe this foe he can face
Seeing them reminds him why he's here in the first place

He stands to his feet, just as the bell sounds
Now he knows what to do
In the second round.

—November 21st, 2011. 1:32a.m.

BITCHES

I saw two mongrels taking a stroll
Shaggy little dogs out in the cold
I was sitting in my car and I watched them dash
Looking at me like they wanted some cash
Picked up by owners they never ever met
To be used and abused worse than any normal pet
Abandoned in the streets, out in the cold
Are those two little mongrels, taking a stroll.

—August 9th, 2011. 11:34pm.

MORNING

Woke up half dazed
My sleep was interrupted by my energetic mind
Woke up listening to steady wisdom
Wisdom that can be hard to find
Wife slept well, she knows when not to think
Watched her mumble in her sleep, talking to spirits I couldn't see
Peaceful murmurs as she slept peacefully
But I stayed up thinking
My body tried to rest but my mind vetoed
It questioned why there were too few hours in the day
Daytime spent working, no time for play
Personal dreams to accomplish, visions it wanted to share
Ideas it wanted to discuss, but my body just didn't care
So I stayed up, with my personal dilemma
Smiling at the beautiful parts that make up me
Staring at my wife
As she slept peacefully.

—*April 12th, 2011. 8:07a.m.*

BEN HINSON

THE SYSTEM

The world is now global
Not understanding this line
Equates to being left behind
See those so called poor countries
Currently taking up less than two percent
Of global economies
Some nations unite; they want bites no more licks
Friends down south qualify to join them and lay BRICKS
Investors want to come in; a few arrive with large sums
They make deals worth billions, cash not seen by anyone
Governments spending millions to impress,
In others we see officials steal the cash
So they stress
No jobs around so people cry
Armed robbers strike and people die
Close marking at the airport, "what did you bring for me?"
Investors don't show up, money likes to travel peacefully
GDP below the mark, they can't place their bets
They did not invest in industry, a decision they'll regret
None of their own have the skill sets or the technology to move ahead
So they pay high rates for foreign companies to do the jobs instead
Kids in structures meant to be schools
No money so the teachers leave the kids to be fools
Young kids taking exams their brains are not trained to take
The future of these nations is truly at stake
The privileged ones get schooling in private academies
Schooling abroad afterwards you can be sure is guaranteed
Can't rely on the private sector to generate jobs in their cities
That's like putting makeup on an ugly face and calling the face pretty

Their faces don't share the same unique vision
Everyone out for themselves, they don't
know the nation's mission
War, war, war, nothing but stupid ethnic divides
Cover ups for monopolizing resources their nation's carry inside
Economies globally connected
Violence on gas lines in one place leaves
everyone affected
Resources not shared
Greed and its child corruption cause despair
The ripple effect is clear
Citizens leave their homes to be immigrants elsewhere
Thinking that their lives will be better
But where they go may even give them worse weather
Conventions had to discuss the times
Authors from these places invited to speak their minds
For a round of loud applause
But the system doesn't care about their cause

—*December 3rd, 2011. 7:07p.m.*

KING

I am a king.

I may not have the accolades but I feel it deep within

My royal blood comes from my state of mind

My appointment is all part of God's design

My confidence is what makes me great

My insecurities make every man relate

I come from nothing so the sky's the limit

I think in big numbers, not in digits

I approach and command attention

Not from appearance but from my disposition

Both the rich and the poor see a friend

I am the same man when dealing with all of them

Like Joseph it's all been planned

Like Menelik I've made my stand

And when the time comes I will shine

I'm being trained now to use my mind

You won't see me on any fancy throne

I'll be with my people or on my own

It won't matter how I leave this place

But it will matter how I run this race

I am a king.

—*April 28th, 2011*

JACKIE

Peaceful woman sitting there
She has many smiles and loves to share
Even through hurts she still remains strong
Her heart is pure and contains no wrong

Peaceful woman sitting there
The chaos comes but she does not care
Her words are few but mean so much
She's friends with God and keeps in touch

And as the world goes by she sits and stares
She takes the time to show she cares
Passing the time with no despair
Is that peaceful woman sitting there.

—*January 31st, 2010. 2:00p.m.*

NEW YORK

6'a.m. and the alarm yells my name
Stayed up late last night playing all my video games
Stare in the bathroom mirror and I see my twin
Then take a shower and wash away the previous day's sins
Walk outside to the street that serves as my yard
I'll be travelling via subway so I'll need a metro card
Dunkin Donuts serves me breakfast every morning
Rush hour traffic so you know the ride will be boring
Get out at 42nd and I get the paper to read
Terrorist threat alert today – just what I need
Walk past the bums and the pimps at the station
Human traffic I see made of people from every nation
I have to make my rounds and hit a few boroughs
So much to do today – can't put it off till tomorrow
Get off the subway and I'm downtown by Wall Street
Turns out there's a client here that I have to meet...
I walk through nothing but suits and high heels
Some walking to their desks and some walking to make deals
Some carrying briefcases, and some wearing gold rings
It's like seeing many twins all doing the same things
Next I hit Union Square, nothing but parks and shops here
I take a break to sit on a bench and then I choose to stare
I see supermodels shaking their hips with long legs like sticks
And also wannabe chicks hoping they too get picked
An old friend of mine texts me, it seems he's in town
He's up in the Bronx so I head up there to Boogie Down
We grab a bite to eat and then I have to go
Head to the Apollo in Harlem and I choose to watch a show
I get a call on my cell, I'm needed in Queens
I take the train past Queensbridge so I can be seen

It seems I made my rounds and hit my mark
So I head down to Brooklyn, Prospect Park
Barbecue scent in the air, seems there is a party going on
Boys and girls chatting when its sex they want all along
Now it's evening and I'm the city, guys I know ask what's happening
I respond and suggest that we all go Meat Packing
While we're there a friend gets ignored and he doesn't understand
Turns out what he thought was a woman was really a man
When that's over I'm back on the subway
A Graffiti sign I see tells me that my day's been okay
Exit the train and I'm back in midtown
Too many tourists here walking aimlessly around
Spot a trader in a truck selling some Halal meat
I haven't eaten all day so I buy a gyro to eat
As I eat I spot a man walking just like I did
Suddenly he gets jumped by a bunch of stick up kids
One trips him up while the other steals his cash
They throw up gang signs and then they dash
I shake my head and keep it moving as the man gets up in a daze
This is new for tourists so they look on amazed
I'm trying to catch a train, but a ticket I can't get
Police have sectioned off the station: looks like a bomb threat
Big crowd gathers around but I'm just trying to get out of town
I ask a cop for options, but he just looks at me with a frown
So I walk around the corner to catch a bus at this time
I get there and I find that there's a really long line
A crazy dude walks up to me and asks if I want to grapple
I politely tell him no so in return he offers me a Big Apple
He won't go away and I have nothing to say
So I put on my headphones and concentrate on my wordplay

I'm on the bus now and see New York's skyline I know
It's feels as if I'm looking at a man made rainbow
Looking through the window at the skyline so pretty
Oh how I love New York City.

—*November 25th, 2011. 9:55p.m.*

MASKS

Public opinions affect the motive
Even the man who goes out of his way to say he doesn't care
By himself sheds a tear
Polite words used at meetings
Masks worn as they give their greetings
Sweet tones that go with dealings
Hard faces when they really have feelings
It's all a game
Which is what makes it a shame
One big costume party
Clothes called clean when they're dirty
Acting becomes the task
Can't come to the party without their Janus masks
Taking it off can be hard on a man
As the mask itself makes demands
This is why unique men are an anomaly
Not understood by much of society
They show up to the party without any masks on
For that they get chastised, ridiculed and scorned
Fear ruling many minds
Mental prisons where they're all doing time
While life goes on
By design.

—*April 27th, 2011. 11:47p.m..*

LOSER

Muscles aching, mental fatigue

Didn't prepare to perform the way he needs

Down on one knee, beaten and broken

Reactions not sharp, defenses open

They cheer for his opponent while he looks and stares

Pride broken, heart shedding tears

He will not understand right away what he's just done

That he faced three challenges while his opponent faced just one

His opponent won the match that put him on top

But he had to fight and lose, and then get back up.

—*September 20th, 2011. 9:24pm.*

SKIN

Little baby, innocent smiles
Mind not corrupted, won't be for a while
The embodiment of beauty, its emotions all true
It sees the heart of men, doesn't judge what they do
Doesn't see them through the skin they wear
Black or white, green or yellow - little baby just doesn't care
Growing up now, placed in different situations
Varied influences, may even live in different nations
Mind fed all sorts of different opinions
Either taught to love or hate
In a conscious or subconscious state
All based on the color of a man's skin
Looking at the packaging and not what's within
Name's made for differences
It shouldn't but it puts up fences
Judging on the package and not the essence
Generations raised with this mental pretense
Communities even, no wise man can be found
A bunch of dummies walking around
Causing trouble, hurting lives
Denying opportunities because of pride
Little baby, once wise with innocent eyes
All grown up, taught to love or despise
Unlearned the template God placed within
Taught to judge a man based on the color of his skin

—August 6th, 2011. 6:15pm

PEACE

Restless mind
Internal prisoner, she's doing time
Carnal nature, emotions dependent on surroundings
Devil knows the switch to turn smiles into crying
Can't sleep at night, she tosses and turns
Perceived offenses; anger burns
Holds on to actions, what others do
When you die my friend, there's no one but you
Insecurity abounds, she asks for opinions
Cares too much what they think, gives up dominion
Depressive spirit, she brings everything down
Wonders later, why no one's around
Used by schemers; they kill her goals
They figure her patterns, consume her soul
Destroy her mind by using her time
Sick in her spirit even though she once was fine
How did she get here? The answer profound
She placed her joy in the tangibles around
And she will stay this way and surely go insane
Till she grows in her spirit, and matures in her brain.

—October 12th, 2011. 4:12p.m.

PERCEPTIONS

Think he's inferior just because he's black
Assumptions made on ignorance, not made on facts
Label him a racist just because he's white
Goldfish called a shark; can't compare their bites
African thinks I'm weak because I'm brown skinned
He doesn't know that in fact I may be harder than him
Call her a slut just because she flirts
She may be a virgin waiting for her first
They laugh and call him a fool because he talks slow
In reality his lips can't capture all his brain knows
They assume he's weak because he doesn't train
They overlook the potential of his human brain
Label him arrogant because he's his own man
His brand of confidence they can't understand
She won't date him because he's poor in the present
But in this life fortunes can change in a moment
Mismanaged perceptions based on conditioning
Illogical rules and senseless reasoning
Assessing on face value, not on potential
Devalued the subject, shame it's intentional.

—*November 11th, 2011. 12:00a.m.*

SEARCH ENGINES

Modern world, data is blood
Queries pour over the web like floods
Nerds are kings, millions made
Tough guys look cool but they don't get paid
The information age, multiple saviors
Complex algorithms control human behavior
Monopolies exist behind the scenes
Smaller companies can't live up to their dreams
The competition speaks without a voice
The dominant players control consumer choice
Content used without permission
Power and money control key decisions
Vertical markets among the few
Senate hearings for points of view
The average consumer doesn't get the situation
Status as pawns in a much bigger equation
Playing monopoly and rolling the dice
Consumers pick up the tab and pay the price.

—*November 5th, 2011. 12:55a.m.*

C TRAIN UPTOWN

So many faces that come and go
On this metal snake that winds through this city that grows
Pretty girl standing next to me wearing a shirt that says enigma
Smiling as she reads a book on AIDS and defeats the stigma
Guy to my right is smiling right at me
He could be gay or maybe just happy to be
Past Fulton street when a musician comes near
He plays with feeling for an audience that doesn't care
Tips his hat and asks for money when he's done with his session
He walks by a homeless man sleeping next to his possessions
A bunch of people board at the Canal street station
One of them is a religious man yelling about his religion
He tells us all that the world is coming to an end
To repent of our sins, and make Jesus our friend
Past West 4th and people board that have me intrigued
One of them is a corporate stiff with his colleagues
He's bragging how he showed some balls to a boss he seethes
With his tight pants one has to ask how his balls can breathe
On to 34th otherwise known as Penn Station
I get off and walk through traffic from every nation
Walk through the tunnels that are this station's veins
To the next platform to catch the next train.

—*June 9th, 2011. 11:07pm.*

RANDOM THOUGHTS...

My Chocolate Covered Peanuts

I'm addicted to them so I chew and chew
Eating my peanut and sugar stew
I know too much is bad but I can't stop my jaws
I eat them all without a pause
Now I'm sitting by myself clutching my stomach in pain
And tomorrow I'll be back eating these damn things again

Spoken Word Jams at the Nubian Palace

Emotional people come here to speak with passion
Expressing their feelings to people who care
Man on stage speaking out about his sexual preference
I block my ears but the women here give him reverence
Then I'm called to the stage because it's my turn to play
But I stand with a blank face because I have nothing to say

—July 18th 2011. 10:48p.m.

WARRIOR

Not every man has the guts to step on the mat
Or in the ring, one on one
Facing another just as tough
Heavy breathing, it's been rough
Hits to the ribs, looking for chokes
Ground positions, going for broke
Back on your feet, he's looking at you
Watching your movements, everything you do
Muscle fatigue, your body wants to quit
You want power, this training makes you fit
Time to see if you were paying attention
Coach's instructions, lesson retention
You watch your opponent
Don't let fear spoil your game
Just remember my friend
He's also thinking the same.

—*August 27th, 2011. 11:59p.m.*

NEW YORK PLAYBOY

Uptown, downtown

Meatpacking, Union Square

Hotel rooftops, designer suits

Top button open, trying to look cute

Thursday night outings, not a care in this life

Making good money, no kids, no wife

Friday night, Saturday night, reliving the same dream

Female lions in the pack pick up the scent of his theme

Spending hundreds every night, maybe even more

Impressing people who don't care who he is at the core

Living the good life, or so it would seem

Let's hope he's ready when it's time to wake up from his **dream.**

—*August 29th, 2011. 9:14pm.*

BEAUTIFUL MUSIC

Smooth, chill, beautiful beats...
Music that stimulates your soul
Giving your emotions a natural high
Tunes that achieve their goal
In my imagination, if God had a pair of headphones
This is what I would picture Him listening to
If I could meet Him for a chat
Listening to this is what we would do
Music this beautiful has to be from heaven
Delivered to us on occasion
Through very special people
With very simple souls
Very simple people
With very special goals
I love this music... the way it makes me feel is indescribable
I cannot put it into words, all I can do is nod
...and look absurd
Listening to the same song repeatedly
Hypnosis I submitted to willingly
Music that evokes peace in me
Beautifully.

—December 17th, 2009. 10:17p.m.

WANNABE RAPPER

A strange thing happened to me the other day
I tried to rap but I couldn't rhyme the right way
I couldn't seem to get in the zone
I couldn't rap, because naturally I sound monotone
I had the words but not the delivery
I caught a classic case of lyrical misery
So I stepped back, relaxed and assessed all the facts
My resume didn't suggest rapping as my main act
So I worked on my pace and my errors I stitched
Stepped up to the mike again and presented my pitch
But the music didn't agree no matter how hard I tried
So I knelt right there in the studio and broke down and cried
And when I finally accepted that this game just wasn't for me
I felt lighter in my spirit because I was finally free.

—June 30th, 2011. 8:13am.

OPPORTUNITY

You are a slick trickster
A popular figure we all want to befriend
You play with emotions, and tease with your offers
But then you disappear, again and again
I search and call your name, but you blatantly ignore my calls
I cry my heart out by your doorstep, but you remain silent behind
your walls
I run my fastest after you, but I can't seem to match your pace
You laugh as I take the defeat and lose this round in our long race
And then I fall into misfortune and curse the day I was born
I curse you with all my might and hang my head low with scorn
And at that moment you show up, and slip in through the back door
Unknown to me you stand and watch as I lay broken on the floor
You quietly grin and hand me a note as I look up in dismay
Turns out my pain was your gift all along, and your note says "it'll be
okay"
You hold me up with a smile on your face and you tell me to look
around
My hard work from chasing you has given me solid ground
You tip your hat and hand me another note as you slowly walk away
"I let you have this round" you say, "but we will race another day."

—September 15th, 2010. 2:22a.m.

MY RESUME

When my mother gave birth to me
For a split second when I was left alone in the nursery
An angel stood by my side where I could see
Whispered in my ear what my legacy would be
While kids played games I wrote ideas
A child doing things most adults wouldn't dare
Spent enough time on my own to devise plans
Before I became a teenager I was already a man
I've earned my stripes for sure
Whether it's the traditional route
Or hustling right out the door
Degrees earned, college hours invested
Corporate gigs, free time rejected
Also sold books like crack on the street
Door to door sales whether snow or in the heat
Manhattan, Washington Heights, Brooklyn... I've walked through them all
Carried my backpack filled with books
As I stopped by every stall
List in my hand of all the stores to hit
Walked through Harlem and the Bronx as I prepared my pitch
Selling my product through my company
Involved in every step in producing what you see
Not to mention all the people that now work for me
I've worked white collar with some of the best brains designed
I've also worked overnight loading trucks for nothing but a dime
Worked at moving companies with ex-convicts
Under the table gigs - no other way for them to get paid
Waiting on the foreman after the job for the money that we made
I respect the human element, because I understand it how it goes

Today I advise clients because they like what I know
I ran against the wind with only God by my side
Too many times rejected, blows to my pride
Had to encourage myself daily because nobody else would
They may be able to help, but they don't think that they should
This is my resume: to followers it may sound cocky and insane
But true leaders will get me, because game recognizes game
Take this as a hint that I'm certified to write this
I live in reality, I don't exist in bliss
My experience makes me the best candidate for your mind
So you can be sure this experience will not be a waste of your time

—December 18th, 2011. 4:20p.m.

HARD GUY

Naïve perceptions in the public eye
Of what it means to be a hard guy
Thug this, armed robber that
He sold drugs, he sold crack
He can probably beat the system
But force him into a tight position
And mentally he goes into remission
Anyone can pose as a tough guy, till they take all of life's tests
May pass one challenge
But then he'll fail the rest
Can pose as a hard guy as long as he doesn't fall into any real traps
Watch him run his mouth till he receives one of Life's bitch slaps
Now he has to deal with a situation
And he sees no way out
Its then that we see what being a hard guy
Is really all about.

—*August 2nd, 2011. 11:59am.*

JUST CHILLIN'

Listening to this beautiful beat, man I'm chillin'
Problems out there but nothing that I'm missing
I love my life and I love the way I live
I love my wife and my soon to be born kid
I love coming home after working for my purse
At least I have a job, it really could be worse
I love taking notes as I sit by the PC
Looking at my faint reflection, yup that's me!
I love being inspired, even when I'm tired
Chatting with God about ideas that get me wired
I love doing things the right way...
You could say every day for me is a good day
I love my possibilities that I can feel
Intangible concepts that I will soon make real
I don't need outside company to feel this good
Opinions don't matter even though some say they should
Chillin' like this is how I love to spend my time
They ask if I'm okay and I reply "I'm just fine."

—July 27th, 2002. 10:00p.m.

FANTASY

When I used to be a dreamer
Relaxed mind state in my chilled house
Before Life decided to get acquainted with me
When I was younger, selfish and carefree
You were my fantasy
Charming smiles, seductive eyes
Elegant charm, the perfect prize
I was a salesman, perfect pitches at the bar
Flirting with you, exchanging smiles from afar
Seen you in London, Accra, so many different places
Even met you in New York, you have so many different faces
Enjoying your attention while corrupting myself
Mental obsessions bad for my health
Temporary sensations not meant to last
One of those demons from my past
Couldn't get enough as there were so many of you
Being a shape shifter is just what you do
Fed my ego as my mind did not grow
Held back in so many ways that I did not know
Took me a while to get over you, but here I am
Gave up my position being your number one fan
You were a drug and now I'm sober
Time freed to live my life before it's all over
But I'll have to watch myself as I mature with what I see
Because I know whenever I look back
You'll be right there waiting for me.

—September 4th, 2011. 9:26pm.

FAKE MO'FO

Can never look a man straight in the eye
Fake smiles even when he tries
Present an achievement and watch his sarcastic grin
Belittles with jokes because he wishes it was him
He'll go after a lover you used to keep
The reason is simple: his game is weak
He'll talk about you yet smile in your face
He knows himself that he's a disgrace
His presence is a stench that is bad for your health
He's the devil's pawn; he has no knowledge of self
The king's among us spot him in a flash
Call him out quick and then watch him dash
Like a rat that runs to hide when the lights' turned on
On the chessboard he falls first because he's just a pawn.

—*September 27th, 2011. 11:32pm.*

BEN HINSON

I LEARN

You never know when what you learn will come into play
Life is unpredictable, we never know past today
I used to work for nothing, pushing heavy loads in cargo bays
I read books on software, more than tripled my daily pay
I researched the arts so I can talk with art dealers
Studied accounting principles so I can talk with book keepers
Studied economics so I can assess the times
Self taught poetic verse – I know I can rhyme
Learned from listening to people with PHDs while in board meetings
Now I'm the one doing the talking while the clients do the listening
I've done research for novels - read journals and study sheets
I've interrogated cops and learned how drugs move on the streets
I've studied martial arts and the many things our bodies can do
Muscle mechanics and physics that can make any man submit to you
I've learned about human nature and the different degrees of people
Some good, many confused and many more that are evil
I learn things really fast – I had to, to get over
I don't need weed to think – I'm high when I'm sober
I've learned so many things, and I'm still learning
A journeyman in this game doing nothing but searching
Taking it all in because I am a king
Doing my best so I don't miss a thing.

—*August 11th, 2011. 1:22pm.*

NERD

There he is, thinking that he's really smart
He's got the brain power but lacks growth with his heart
Numbers and trends give him sweet sensations
His thoughts revolve around nothing but binary equations
Limited thinking keeps him around his own kind
He gets the brain but doesn't understand the human mind
Believes what could be as present reality
So in a sense he more than anyone lives in a fantasy
Laws of science, other's theories take his slots
His mind a scatter chart and his soul can't connect the dots
Quantum physics, good attempt at understanding spirits
Mathematically inclined, not many care for this skill
So he finds them all stupid, because they choose their own will
Arrogance multiplied, in his nerd outfit it's disguised
But we see right through him
His armor of definitions is too thin
Who cares what song he sings
When he's dead his theories won't mean a thing
And that can happen at any time
Forecasts don't always predict the next day's true design
So we drink our wine while he wastes his mind
Shake our heads as we watch him waste his time.

—*September 23, 2011. 12:39am.*

PEACEFUL

Peaceful, like watching a loving father talk to his new-born son;
Peaceful, like sitting on the beach and watching the waves beat the
shore...
Peaceful, like reading a book you love for so long,
Peaceful, like watching a starving child being fed, ask for more.
Peaceful, like daydreaming of your love as a gentle breeze is blowing...
Peaceful, like being asleep and dreaming about all the things you
adore.
Peaceful, like watching the rain as it continues falling;
Peaceful, like being in love and not asking for anything more

Peaceful...that's me.

—*May 17th 2003, 2:08am.*

RANDOM THOUGHTS...

<u>White collar work:</u>
No time for breakfast
And hardly any sleep, especially as I work on my dreams...outside of
the white collar routine
But hopefully it will pay off, all this time I give
Because I don't live to work, but I work to live

<u>Coffee</u>
I hate it
But I think I need it to function
Looking at numbers, making decisions
Lack of sleep puts my attention in remission
Funky breath it gives for keeps
A painful reminder that I need some sleep

<u>Sparring</u>
My favorite form of exercise
Learning technique and how to attack; I used to push weights but
they didn't push back
Repetitive moves build muscle mechanics
Being taught how to control my pace and not panic

<u>Smiling</u>
I have to admit, I used to be a mean dude
Never smiled, perceptions I was rude
But it's amazing the things a smile can do: positive aura draws
people to you
Now I try to smile, even when I'm feeling down - a former grump
who's now a clown.

—*July 18th 2011. 4:15p.m.*

BEN HINSON

THE GRAVEYARD

Slow cold steps through this quiet place
Wasted potential in this dark space
All the dead here no more can see
Some never became what they were meant to be
Buried dreams and unfulfilled destinies
Guilty of committing spiritual felonies
Books never written, paintings never painted
Songs never sang, creations never created
Goals never accomplished, ideas never enacted
Mostly because in life the wrong things kept them distracted
Peer pressure, fear, slaves to selfish visions
Walking the wrong way, making bad decisions
A few stand out; tombstones looking new
They died with nothing else in this world left to do
Life didn't stop them, resolve never diminished
Like Jesus they could say in the end "it is finished."
But some laying here can't make such claims
The world moves on and no one remembers their names.

—October 5th, 2011. 11:47p.m.

MY BROTHER

It's amazing the bond we share
Bloodlines have no effect on the bond we have here
We connect because we relate to each other
We're not blood yet you are my brother
I can talk to you about anything on my mind
Whenever we meet it's truly quality time
I enjoy you because you truly understand
Two kings, conversing and making plans
The depth you bring to our meetings is profound: I've conversed
with many minds but none with your sound
Whenever we part ways I learn something new
Two men who respect each other's points of view
I feel God put you on my path to help me grow
Your intentions are pure and in your actions it shows
You're not pretentious and you don't hold back
You're the right combination of emotion and facts
You don't share others business when we chat
I trust you because I know that you're not a rat
Opinions don't affect our bond that is efficient
Time apart doesn't matter: your maturity keeps you consistent
The most important asset in life, time, you share
Whenever I need you physically you're always there.

— July 31st, 2011. 10:43pm.

WEAPONS

I've held a sawed off shotgun and fired at targets
Held a Beretta Cheetah, felt its cold steel in my hand
I've seen knife play, and had a blade pointed at me
I've seen what a baseball bat can do to a man's memory
I've trained in martial arts, learned how to subdue a man with skill
I've trained with seasoned fighters with hands licensed to kill
Wondered which weapon was the most powerful by design
When I realized the most powerful of them all was my <u>mind</u>.

—*April 28th 2011, 12:50a.m.*

TOKEN

Single kid growing up in a single household
No father figure there to mold
Can't use that as an excuse, others have made it
And much worse, different mind states
Guess this is a subject we can debate
Coming up strong, propaganda received
He just chooses the wrong thing to believe
The hood is on the other side of town
Daily trips because its thugs he wants to be around
Baggy jeans sagging showing their underwear
Calling cards for sex between the men here
But they don't even know it, and he doesn't know it too
A shame all the things that a lost mind can do
Now he's moving with new friends
Forget about school, he wants to be like them
Subconscious peer pressure affects his personality
Single mother does her best to try and help him see
Many nights crying, she tells him to stay home
But his pride speaks up and he leaves her all alone
Hanging out with bad men who use him to do bids
Instead of school he's learning how to be a stick up kid
The promise was there but he threw it away
Legacy knocked on his door but he wanted to play
He's just a shard in a system that's broken
Like a black man in a white flick he's just a token
Now he pledges allegiance to his new brothers
Check him out now, he's wearing their colors
Stability traded for fast cash and drugs
His mother wants to hold her son but he's not there for hugs
Friends he had now with jobs, investing and saving

He spends his money on new sneakers and brand name clothing
Run-ins with the law; arrested with mother crying at the door
Unnecessary drama, one wonders what the heck for?
Grown man now but he still thinks like a child
Some of his friends have calmed down but he's still acting wild
But Life catches up to him
Gives him a quick bitch slap and an upside down grin
Can't jump people his whole life, he needs a job instead
So self involved, doesn't even realize his mother is dead
It seems reality did not agree with his fantasies
He works minimum wage and he's not at ease
He sees a way out in music and becoming a rapper
Grown man with kids half his age on the block spitting Cyphers
On the side he may sell weed or maybe crack cocaine
Our people are suffering and he's just adding to the pain
Bumps into old friends he went to school with,
Ducks and decides to see them later
They look good and he's jealous which means he's now a hater
Life has moved on, even former gang bangers he knew are all gone
Its then he realizes in this game he's been the dummy all along
Depression sets in, can't deal with it sober
He needs something quick to take the pain over
The bottle doesn't help, and weed only makes the thoughts worse
Cocaine makes him restless, and together they take up his purse
Cord around the arm, he cooks up the black tar
Shoots it up the vein, the heroin goes really far
This new addiction of his takes all his money
People see him and shake their heads because he's now a junkie
Moving through crack houses, anywhere for a fix
Sharing needles with strange people, HIV in the mix

Stealing here and there to get by
Even putting food on the side to get high
Cops arrive on the scene, 911 was their alarm
Find Token dead on a chair, cord tied to his arm

— *December 21st, 2011. 3:21a.m.*

BEN HINSON

SINGLE STORY

Wishing for more wisdom,
Proper application to make more informed decisions
Rather than seeing things through just one dimension
Wishing to have explored the options and asked more questions

Minds full of assumptions and half truths
Stereotypes ruling whole worldviews
Puppets walking with corrupted perceptions
Wasted minds with no sense of direction

Been taught to see only one side of what they've done
Repeatedly told the same story till that's what they become
Told a story that strips them of what they can be
When in reality the similarities go beyond what most can see.

— *December 13th 2010, 3:04am.*

THE FUTURE

Whatever happens, happens
Working hard for goals, but life's intangibles are there
Seeing others with no peace, stressed out, losing their hair
I want to make it big and have money so I can function
I don't love money my friend, but I do like having options
So I'm not going to hold on tightly to dreams that may not be
I'll work hard towards what I love, and be at peace with what I see
Neither my problems nor the future defines me
I don't deal in dreams but in reality
Takes some time for a man to get to this stage
Takes some humbling and maturing for a man to act like his age
No man can see the future, and anything can happen
Dreams are crushed daily, unpredictable distractions
So I'll say by God's grace, what will be will be
I want to be a big baller, but I'm just as happy being me
I'll work my hardest at what I love, and do it well before I die
Because tomorrow is not guaranteed, and all I can do is try.

—*August 16th, 2011. 11:40pm.*

PAIN

I now see better, like a weatherman who gets the weather
I've been through fire, had my initiation to grow
I'm in a secret brotherhood, most of its members even I don't know
We talk a certain way, think along distinct lines
What others complain about we see as just fine
Training received to take the mind beyond intellectual limitations
Learned to understand and fathom intangible situations
Moved away from know it alls: nothing in them ever died
Arrogance and assumptions made, this is nothing but pride
Necessity forces a man to see resources differently
No luxury there to criticize others,
Has to worry about his own security
I opened a bank account, listed my experience in my budget
In my balance sheet, listed every crisis as an asset
The intellectual needs his degrees and books as his prize
We're a step beyond that, experienced our pain to be called wise
I embrace pain, even though I never look for it
Smile at the challenge because I'll never quit
Black rock through fire that becomes a gem
They laugh at me but soon I'll be laughing at them.

— *September 11th, 2011. 9:41p.m.*

IGNORANCE

If I knew I could,

But that doesn't mean I would.

And if I fail to change I blame myself for pain.

And I can't hide and say that I did not know,

For the knowledge was given but I did not grow.

—*March 13th 2008, 9:37pm.*

BIG RED BUTTON ON HER FOREHEAD

In this life very few care

About the process involved in getting there

Good or bad, the theory is the same

Assess the woman how she is

Don't care how she became

She flares up in public

Her hot temper the topic

"I know how to destroy her," is what that wicked man said

"All I have to do is push that big red button on her head."

— *November 12th, 2011. 11:51p.m.*

LIFE CHANGES

One of those periods in my past
No money, my little savings just won't last
Just the previous year worked white collar, sat in board rooms
Discussing accounts worth millions, too much too soon
Sitting in meetings with Ivy Leaguers, glass windows over
New York city
Feeling on top of the world, the arrogance seemed to fit me
Traded in my suit for work boots, my filed hands for work gloves
Swapped my fancy talk for street sense, traded work associates
for real friends
Rich lifestyle traded for poverty, a classic lesson from God in humility
But I appreciate that period, and all the others like it
Practical lessons in how fast life can change; tempted to fold,
tempted to complain
Now pennies impress me, I already know how big money is spent
In other words my friends, I learned how to be content
Now I'm back to being a big baller- making more loot
than I ever made
No more work boots, working overnight and physical
feats to get paid
But what I learned in those periods stuck with me, I can't erase it
from my mind
It's worth more than lessons from boardrooms or any school
you can find
It's that extra edge you need to have if you want to pass the test
That extra merit I earned that separates a leader from the rest
The lifestyle that money brings can certainly change a man
So it's good I've lived both sides, so now I understand

BEN HINSON

That who I am is not based on the tangibles that come and go
But rather on the changes in my life that I've come to know.

—July 23rd, 2011. 9:50pm.

LENNY

Past memories
When I was a young nomad going places
Meeting faces
Lenny was there
Met him alone
Two of us on the streets, we roamed
Figuring out life, time on our hands
I knew where I was going, not sure if he had plans
Denied the love, ego starts to fret
Young Lenny soon joins a set
Separate paths, I'm on my way
I've been through much, but that's yesterday
Can't look back, I'll turn to salt
Reliving the past only makes me halt
Old photos I see, Lenny and me
He was my only friend and he was a friend for free
Today I wonder where he stands with his mind
A shame if he's done nothing but waste his time.

—*October 8th, 2011. 4:00a.m.*

WORDPLAY

I really respect the art form of rap
It may seem easy but it's not in fact
At least for a beginner like me
I have the wordplay but not the delivery
I try to match my pace to the beat
It's a tough challenge, an incredible feat
I feel like a man who can't dance easily
That's what this is: dancing lyrically
Spoken word to a precise rhythm
Catchy punch lines for ears that are willing to listen
My childhood spent playing barefoot soccer in Africa
We did this while American kids were spitting Cyphers
They were trained from childhood to be linguists you see
Big Daddy Kane and Nas raised from birth to be MC's.
So for now I'll sit back and do what I do best
Orchestrate my thoughts as if I'm playing chess
I am content being the mastermind as I keep them thinking
Present my propaganda and have them do my bidding
Keep a tight lid with the things that I say
While I construct thoughts to move nations through my wordplay.

—*October 24th, 2011. 6:00p.m.*

HUNGRY

I stood in line, I stood in line, I asked for food but I got declined.
So I stood and wondered why no one cared, I saw them eating but they did not share.
I tried to yell for them to help me out, but I was so hungry that I could not shout.
So I bowed my head and stood in line, and thought about food to pass the time.

—February 22nd 2009. 3:00am.

BREDREN

Back in my country
Third world nation, people are hungry
Old friends I left behind
Not my doing, all God's design
Old friend visits so we chat and bask
He needs cash but his dignity makes him not ask
Tells me about the tough life he's living here
No jobs for him, no money to spare
Armed robbers saw his savings and took it all
No 911 for him to call
No welfare check for him to claim
You can see on his face he's wearing his pain
He doesn't understand why since birth he's been so skint
When he signed the deal with life he forgot to read the small print
I watch his movements and study his words
The fact he's suffering seems so absurd
I pat his back and say what I can to strengthen
Make plans to help because he is my bredren
Make him laugh because it's good medicine for the pain
As I search for a solution deep in my brain.

—July 1st, 2011. 5:52p.m.

KNOWLEDGE INCREASES YOUR CAPACITY TO BE A FOOL

Read the books, he passed the class
Said the prayers, made the mass
Trained with coach to run the race
Lessons learned to watch the pace
Got so much, they all cheered
They believed he truly was in top gear
Hundred degrees yet he chose to be broke
Medical doctor who chose to smoke
Two pieces of fruit sitting in a can
The first called rotten when it understands
Simple man called stupid but he plays it cool
I wonder between the two who is the bigger fool.

—*October 12th, 2011. 12:52a.m.*

FINGERPRINTS

You are irreplaceable
Billions of people on the earth
Billions of smiles and facial tints
But all through it all
Only you have your fingerprints
Original creation, unique sperm formation
Unique ways of filtering thoughts in your station
You are an original, one of a kind
Makes no sense then to imitate others and lose your mind
Realizing your uniqueness is what makes you significant
Trying hard to fit their standards just makes you a replicant
God only makes originals, this is a hint
Billions of models out there, none with your fingerprints.

— *October 14th, 2011. 1:59p.m.*

IMMIGRANT

Trading seasons for different reasons
Leaving homes to be adopted
Ripple effects of colonialism
Bad governance, imperialism
Serial wanderers, moving around
Looking for capital to be found
Playing games and trading places
Signing up to be rats and run rat races
Making transitions that can be hard
Doctors, lawyers now security guards
Cash exoduses, seemingly strange
Keeping economies alive – foreign exchange
Global citizens even though they don't belong
Paid below minimum wage – now that's just wrong
Men and women leaving their nations for new stations
Their sacrifices made for future generations.

—*August 17th, 2011. 10:30pm.*

JERRY

Ben and Jerry, you and me
The closest thing to family
The most material friend I've ever had
I'm the good one and you're just bad
Our tastes in things are radically different
You are a trouble maker that is efficient
You're a failure because you can't take directions
Told to stand at ease yet you stand at attention
You play with my ego and make it seem just fine
Suggest things that are usually a waste of my time
Of all the bad friends I've had you're the worst with peer pressure
You don't care about my well being, all you want is pleasure
The fact that we're friends sometimes makes me scoff
But you're practically like family so I can't just cut you off
So I stay with you, and you stay with me
Attached for life is what it seems to be.

— *October 30th, 2011. 11:05p.m.*

EVENING

Heading back home after a long day
My mind is burnt out and fatigued in the wrong way
Spent the day fueling corporate dreams
Getting paid at work to pledge allegiance to corporate schemes
Sat on a bumpy ride home with the bus jerking
With many workers just like me sitting still thinking
Little kid up front staring right at me
Sitting on her moms lap she can't be more than three
She must see into my spirit because she doesn't look away
She smiles at me and giggles as if she wants to play
I grin as her mother takes her off the bus
I watch them leave thinking soon she may be one of us
Only a few hours left in the day, wondering what to do
The sun laughs at me as it sets and hides from view
Walk in the door and smile as my wife grins
Take a shower and wash away the day's sins
Walk to my kitchen and I get some food
Afterwards fetch my pen and change my mood
Before long my eyes shutter from the fatigue in my brain
In a few hours I'll have to get up and do it all over again.

—*May 30th, 2011. 9:55a.m.*

BUBBLE WITH HARD WALLS

Bubble with hard walls
Is it worth it, really think about it
Educational systems set up
To teach you how to work for others
Processes created
To produce followers and not leaders
Mothers cheering their children
Proud to see them graduate, not caring for their true fate
Even though some can relate
Uneven scales in offices, veterans working like novices
Hardest workers victimized
Work all you want
Middle men will still criticize
So what's the point of it all? Where is God on this corporate call?
Imbalanced intangibles
Soul draining mandibles
Families to feed
So some adhere to their creed
This is the life that they lead, to get illusions they think they need
So many minds trapped in the matrix
A few break out and they make it
But for most this is all
A bubble with hard walls.

—*September 13th, 2011.*

ROSE

A <u>good</u> wife is like a beautiful rose
They say the most beautiful roses come with the worst thorns
And her prickly thorns might just leave you torn
Might be past baggage, might be drama to manage
Might be in-laws who interfere, ex-lovers who just don't care
Jealous friends who do jealous things, even your own family that
might sting
You have a gift from God so the devil will test; he'll use anybody and
won't let you rest
You'll have to resist with all your might, might be even yourself you'll
have to fight
But stay strong my brother and resist the urge
The process reveals what in us we need to purge
It might seem hopeless but every test has its end
The key is that you and your wife remain friends
And when all the thorns are plucked and you've paid your dues
You'll see the beautiful rose that God picked for you.

—March 4th, 2011. 9:16pm.

EDEM

Young man with promise
Immigrant searching for knowledge
Came to America for college
His degree earned and acknowledged

Celebrating his achievement with friends
His day, so its friends that spend
Couldn't see the knucklehead approaching
Knucklehead with his friends loathing

Intentionally bumped into Edem at the bar
Starting trouble, Edem fights like a star
The cowards leave the premises;
Their goal was to make a new nemesis

Edem exits the venue; next day is the graduation ceremony
Mom made some home cooking
Had to get home to celebrate with everybody

Knuckleheads waiting outside, but this time they brought a friend
Cowards run up to Edem, shots fired,
and Edem's life ends

Back at home family waited, but Edem never showed
He was sleeping on the concrete, skin had gone cold

He could have been a father, a brother, an entrepreneur or a hustler
He could have been a good friend, a lover, a president or a scholar

Destroyed potential, family and nation grieving at his wake

His nation needed leaders and he's another candidate
they couldn't take

All because of some cowards who couldn't check their pride
They're not real men, that's why in groups they stride
Edem is gone and we all cry
While I scratch my head and ask myself why.

— *July 31st, 2011. 11:55pm.*

THE FOOLISH MAN

The foolish man lacks direction
Judges the class without taking the lesson
Does not value the pain in change
He's weak in spirit and a child in the brain
He's the first to talk and the last to think
His mind is poor and is not synched
He talks and talks like he knows it all
But listening to him will make you fall
And other fools indeed think he's clever
For birds of the same feather flock together
And he judges a meal without a taste
He goes on looks and acts in haste
And he can't ever seem to understand
That behind everything there is a plan
If only he knew the things we knew
He would talk much less and change his views
But the fool can't seem to understand
His pride is much and it makes demands
And the sad thing is which he doesn't know
Is that he's a fool and it always shows.

—January 3rd, 2009. 11:34pm.

LOVE

Immature mind, never tested
Never had to deal with the uncomfortable, always rested
Wanting things for lustful reasons, selfishness
Only what you can get out of it, recklessness
For you to want it, it has to be a certain way
Mind stuck in pause every single day
Dealing with things and people from a limited view
The mind doesn't function the way God wants it to
Love breaks the bonds and all the stipulations
Love brings the maturity in every situation
Love breaks down the arrogance that comes from pride
Love doesn't see faults and love doesn't hide
Good way to test if you understand the concept
Take something attractive you think you love, be honest
And if all its allure was suddenly taken away
Ask yourself if you would run or if you would stay.

—*August 2nd, 2011. 5:10pm.*

KID

King Solomon's riches, never had to hustle
Never went through the process to understand the game
He learns new moves
But his mind stays the same
Ego always on full blast
His lips move too fast
Life not yet given him a test to pass
And if it has then it means he failed the class
His life experience evident from the things he said
Still a lot of room for wisdom to fit in his head
Doesn't matter his age or what he claims he did
Because it's clear to us that he's just a kid.

—October 26th, 2011. 6:18a.m.

TROUBLE

You wanted to go there but instead ended up here,
Dealing with sudden changes you didn't ask for
You want it to stop but it seems you get more,
And life itself seems like one big chore
Seeing others merry only enhances the pain, illusions put up for you to see
But rest assured that every man has his lot,
His own struggles assigned by his degree
Trouble always comes in one form or another; this is an unfortunate fact of life
You may overcome and do many great things,
But trouble will always be right there in sight
You may lose something physical, mental or financial,
Maybe a fantasy or dream may seem stolen
Your world will be rocked by this sudden change,
In other words trouble will leave your world broken
They key is not whether you try to avoid trouble,
For trouble will find you no matter where you run
But what matters is how you handle trouble,
When your trouble itself finally comes.

—*July 26th, 2011. 11:03pm..*

BEN HINSON

THE MIND

The <u>mind</u> is a priceless weapon
It can do the impossible with the right perception
A dictator's one mind can mobilize millions
With it the Wright brothers flew and brought meaning to the word vision
Through the mind cult leaders have driven many to suicide
Foolish warlords have wasted this priceless weapon through genocide
The mind is the focus of many religions
It's the prize in the battle between angels and demons
The full use of the mind goes beyond intellectual knowledge
It's used in the occult to cause trouble and carnage
It's nourished in clean faiths to bring deliverance from bondage
It can bring internal peace or can keep a free man living as a hostage
It's with the mind that a deformed cripple chooses to smile with pride
It's also through the mind that a person who has it all commits suicide
It's the one thing the vast majority in the middle don't understand
While in the background the forces of good and evil make their plans
The mind is the most important piece of the puzzle called man
A simple fact that mankind has proven it doesn't understand.

—*July 26th, 2011. 11:03pm.*

COCAINE

New York highlife, no cares
Lavish parties, find them there
Suburban minded, families funding housing
They have jobs, nice apartments for lounging
Orgies here
Lines of coke they want to share
Ask me if I'll have some
Shake my head, I'll have none
Buy their ounces, infected nostrils
Sniff up lines with rolled up dollar bills
Back in Ghana no money there
Nigeria, Sierra Leone, gang warfare
Shipments come in at the docks
Headed for Europe and America to buy up stock
Some gets left behind
Not just coke
But drugs of every kind
Heroin and their cousins crack cocaine
Worth much so the streets start to go insane
Armed robbery escalates, crime on the rise
Stability shaken, police demise
Youth see easy money, abandon school for bucks
You'll see the same in any American project that's stuck
Sniffing up the nostrils till all the lines are done
They ask if I'll have some
But I say I'll have none.

—*November 3rd, 2011. 1:34a.m.*

RANDOM THOUGHTS...

Realities of Liberation

It is easier to bring a man out of something
Than to bring that something out of the man.

Hole in my sock

I found a hole in my sock just the other day
My toe stuck out of it and wanted to play
I wore my fancy suit and fancy shoes to a fancy party
And the only one who knew about the hole was me
Now as time went on and we drank our wine
A glass was raised and the host called for time
"Time to play a game," he said in the midst of a cough
And to play we all had to sit down, and take our shoes off

—*October 30th, 2011. 11:23p.m.*

11 KINDS OF PEOPLE YOU'LL MEET IN MOST OFFICES

The man/woman who intentionally
does not respond to your emails. That's okay;
just keep email or paper trails.

The people who walk around most of the day
chatting and wasting time. They are the office radios,
not much work occupying their minds.

The person or people on your team
who ask a million questions.
I say be patient with this group,
it may be they have bad directions.

The annoying coworkers
who make a big deal over trivial situations.
They are drama queens who enjoy
having meaningless conversations.

The office gossips who usually huddle
in groups of three or two.
Wasting valuable productive hours
to sit and talk about you.

The man/woman in a leadership position
that clearly did not earn their label.
Discuss the details and look for feedback
and they are never able.

The traitors that are always close to home,
usually found on your very own team.

Judas wannabe's portraying you in a negative light
whenever you're not on the scene.

The nice person who makes time for you,
that is if you're not a dick yourself.
They take the time to show you the ropes
when no one else offers you help.

The positive folk, humble and hardworking,
if you have a good spirit these are the ones to be around...
they learn what they can and will help you out
when you're feeling down.

The rebels - that bunch that love complaining
just about everything.
They will spend the whole work day sitting in negativity,
complaining and not doing a thing.

And finally there is you.

— *August 26th, 2011. 1:17pm.*

CHANGES

Many walk around without a clue
Changes happen in only a few
Old things will soon pass away
And when changes come changes stay.

And when growth comes you will know
In your actions it will surely show
You might even become confused
Because changes change former views.

And when the spirit changes your body should follow
But the process is rough and may leave you in sorrow
Hence only a few truly understand
The difference a change can make in a man.

— May 21st, 2009. 2:07a.m.

DO YOU BELIEVE

Do you believe, that you can be free
Even though you look
And it seems you can't see

Do you believe, you can overcome
Even though your life
Suggests a different outcome

Do you believe, in who you really are
Even though you feel dirty
And don't feel like a star

Do you believe, the lies you are told
Or do you claim your right
To stand and be bold

Do you believe, in speaking life to your soul
Or do you fold
And keep from reaching your goals

For your destiny in this life, depends on what you believe
And what you receive
Goes with the voices you heed

So pay attention to the voices you hear, the people you see
The words you read
And the life you lead

Then choose to believe, in who you really are
Believe in your purpose
And you will go really far.

—*June 23rd 2009, 1:30am.*

BEN HINSON

LITTLE FINGERS

Little mind should be in school
Instead on a training program to be a fool
Deep rooted traditions while the world moves on
Evolution the world over but here not born
Value of the theme called education not known
Great nations have trees but here no seeds are sown
Counterparts abroad learning history and equations
Brains being nurtured to take the lead in their nations
But here this little mind is stuck in the traffic
Little fingers on the trigger or catching fish like magic
Little fingers against his will mending nets in the sun
He should be schooling with friends, and learning how to have fun
Little fingers can't comment, he has nothing to say
And at the end of the day, it's the nation that pays

— *September 4th, 2011. 11:53pm.*

VEIL

I felt so alone and so depressed
As I thought time wasted away
I worked with the little that I possessed
And did my best to feel okay

As I toiled alone and questioned life
As all my friends seemed to disappear
I kept on working with all my might
And had faith that my God cared

And just when I thought it was all in vain
And a wretch was what I had become
The veil was taken from my eyes
And I saw all that I had done.

—*January 5th 2010, 9:30am.*

TONGUE

Be careful with whom you choose to share
Don't believe everything you get to hear
Data in the wrong hands can be deadly
And not all friends you have are friendly
Even close ones can share your ways
It takes just a big mouth to go astray
The tongue is deadly and does nothing true
A false report can change a point of view
Information shared can go round and round
A snowball effect till it becomes too profound
Talking in the dark about others not there
Assumptions and secrets discussed and shared
So be careful with whom and what you say
Discretion is needed to avoid being prey
Loose lips destroy a great many friendships
And a gossip creates a great many hardships
Pay attention, for these things are true
Take it from us who've learned and paid our dues
The tongue indeed is a deadly weapon
Wise men are quiet and practice discretion.

— *August 7th, 2010. 5:16pm.*

PLASTIC

Hot sweaty weather
Corporations own water supplies
Young girl takes plastic
Bags water for a prize
She sells it on the street
They buy and drink to escape the heat
Don't care for their town
Done drinking, see plastic on the ground
Plastic bags soon fill beyond
Evolve and morph into little ponds
Plastic trash becomes new homes
Mosquitoes breed and start to roam
Self inflicted malaria epidemic
Foreign aid freaks out and starts to panic
Millions spent, nets made to ease the stress
They don't take the time to fully understand process
People dying, people crying
Plastic trash multiplying
Empower the people, no they buy their nets
As the people unknowingly increase their debts

— *October 6th, 2011. 12:17a.m.*

THE ROAD

Idea pops in the head, so you move
That idea bears no fruit, so you improve
Many contacts around
But so few originals to be found
Friend doesn't promote you, because you're not in his heart
Believe me if he really loved you, he would have helped from the
start
It stings being in these scenes
Now you know what maturity really means
Keep on travelling down your narrow road
People will come and people will go
Don't hold grudges on what they do
Doing so is just letting dead weight sink you
Walk down your road and keep a smile as you go
Don't wear any insecurity on your sleeves to show
Push through it all and you'll have a story to tell
Of how you had little help but yet made it through hell
Walk down your road and learn from the scenes
And soon you'll be making real what once were dreams

—*November 12th, 2011. 2:37p.m.*

AFTERMATH

Reverting to traditional methods after they were colonized
Optimization not a vision in their eyes
The world moves forward but they live in the past
Rural areas kept poor and separated by class
Extreme religion and ethnic divisions keeps them divided
The world's global now, seems they were never reminded
Central authorities and the people not connected
Accountability from the leaders never expected
Failed over time to build accountable institutions
The locals smile with foreigners but that's just an illusion
Can't spread the wealth because the wealth's not even built
Corrupt leaders on all levels steal with no guilt
Knuckleheads hate the system so they go to war
Adding problems to an already corrupted core
Colonization ended years ago but it's still the same
Foreign debt keeps these people in nothing but chains
Debt that comes from the above points and no innovation
A vicious cycle that occurs in many of their nations
They need top minds to draft needed constitutions
And character amongst themselves to honor resolutions
New systems needed so their nations can be strong
So they won't stay in place while the world moves along

— *October 27th, 2011. 12:55a.m.*

BEN HINSON

CHUMP

Can't take a man seriously
Who talks about what his plans are
He has no finished product
Yet he wants to be a star
You've done all the hard work
All behind the scenes
He comes and says "let's do something"
He wants to be part of your dream
Assess a man by what he does, not by claims on what he can do
No finished product he can present
Then he shouldn't be talking to you

—November 6th, 2011. 1:41a.m.

FABRIC OF SOCIETY

Few minds functioning
Majority of the switches turned off
Zombies walking around breathing
Potential trouble breeding
All it takes is an evil visionary
Just one needed to be the emissary
One mind starts the propaganda
Needed to plant the desire
One mind lights the candle
And the knuckleheads start the fire
The puppet master pulls his strings
Dummies walk around and do bad things
Such a thin fabric that holds it all together
Intellectual arrogance tears at the tether
Love is the medicine that we all need
That and education to plant good seeds
Negative spirits working hard to corrupt
Men and their minds to self destruct.

—*September 4th, 2011. 11:18pm.*

ORIGINAL

He's an original, one of a kind
Being a wordsmith is in his design
Transferred his African skill sets as a linguist
If writing was a drug trade, he would be a chemist
He is a certified professional that's intentional
He writes most of his pieces to beats that are exceptional
He's been through Pete Rock's treasures and plundered
He's spent time observing the world's 9th wonder
No odd words in his wordplay, his words are even
His words impregnate ideas like a woman filled with semen
He prefers not to freestyle, he likes to think before he talks
Gives visible lessons like a blackboard gets from chalk
He's an original, one of a kind
Imitations see his words and they use his lines
He mixes words like a bartender does drinks
Fancy cocktails of thought that make you think
He says these lines to a crowd and they can't help but listen
They get amazed at how his piece was carefully written
Each word selected to plant a seed in their brains
When he's done believe me they'll not be the same
His words get done and they ask for more
And he can deliver because there's so much in store
They don't regret it's with him that their time is spent
Because they know this is a once in a lifetime event
He's an original, like no one does he try to be
In a garden with plants he's a tree
Not arrogant by any means, rather confident and eclectic
His life used to be an act, but now he's authentic
He steps into a room and they know a leader is there
Evident by the way some of them stop and stare

Others hate his glare, why he wonders
But God is on his side, so no weapons shall prosper
He knows himself well, that makes him a confident individual
In a room full of copies, he's an original.

—November 9th, 2011.

••••

For more information on the Chapters of Me series,
please join the page at:
facebook.com/ChaptersOfMe
For more information on Ben Hinson, please visit:
www.benhinson.com
And on Facebook:
facebook.com/BenHinson2
You can also follow Ben on Twitter here:
http://twitter.com/BenHinson

For direct/bulk orders, please contact Musings Press:

Musings Press
P.O Box 8718
New York, NY. 10116
Tel: 201.453.3929

For booking information and press inquiries, please contact
LaDawn Michele at ladawn@benhinson.com

MUSINGS PRESS™

CPSIA information can be obtained at www.ICGtesting.com
Printed in the USA
LVOW12s1528300314

379492LV00003B/108/P